Colour Plate 1   Titian, *Mary Magdalen*, *c.*1567, oil on canvas, 128 × 103 cm, Capodimonte Museum, Naples. *Photo*: Scala, Florence.

Colour Plate 2   Artist unknown, *Pantocrator, Angels, the Virgin and the Apostles*, 12th century, mosaic, Cefalu Cathedral, main apse. *Photo*: Scala, Florence.

Colour Plate 3 Gianlorenzo Bernini, *Triton* fountain, 1642–3, travertine, Piazza Barberini, Rome. *Photo*: Scala, Florence.

Colour Plate 4   Claes Oldenburg, *Feasible Monument for a City Square : Hats Blowing in the Wind*, 1969, canvas, wire, starched with glue, painted with spray enamel, mounted on wood base, shellacked, 27 × 71 × 99 cm, detail, Manilow Collection. *Photo* : Tate Gallery, London.

Colour Plate 5 Raphael, *Solly Madonna*, *c*.1500, oil on panel, 52 × 38 cm, Staatliche Museen Preussischer Kulturbesitz (Gemäldegalerie), Berlin. *Photo*: Jörg P. Anders.

Colour Plate 6   Raphael, *Tempi Madonna*, 1507–8, oil on panel, 75 × 52 cm, Alte Pinakothek, Munich. *Photo*: Blauel/Gnamm–Artothek.

Colour Plate 7   Raphael, *Niccolini-Cowper Madonna* or *Large Cowper Madonna*, 1508, oil on wood, 81 × 57 cm, Andrew W. Mellon Collection, National Gallery of Art, Washington.

Colour Plate 8 Benjamin West, *The Death of General Wolfe*, 1770, oil on canvas, 151 × 213 cm, National Gallery of Canada, Ottawa. Gift of the Duke of Westminster.

Colour Plate 9   Hieronymus Bosch, *Tabletop of the Seven Deadly Sins and the Four Last Things*, *c.*1400, oil on panel, 120 × 150 cm, Prado Museum, Madrid. *Photo:* Scala, Florence.

Colour Plate 10   Hendryk van Steenwyck, *Still-life : an Allegory of the Vanities of Human life*, c.1620–30, oil on oak panel, 39 × 51 cm, National Gallery, London.

Colour Plate 11   Thomas Gainsborough, *Mr and Mrs Andrews, c.*1749, oil on canvas, 70 × 120 cm, National Gallery, London.

Colour Plate 12   Nicolas Poussin, *Landscape with the Body of Phocion Carried out of Athens*, 1648, oil on canvas, 114 × 175 cm, Collection of the Earl of Plymouth. *Photo*: courtesy of the National Museum of Wales.

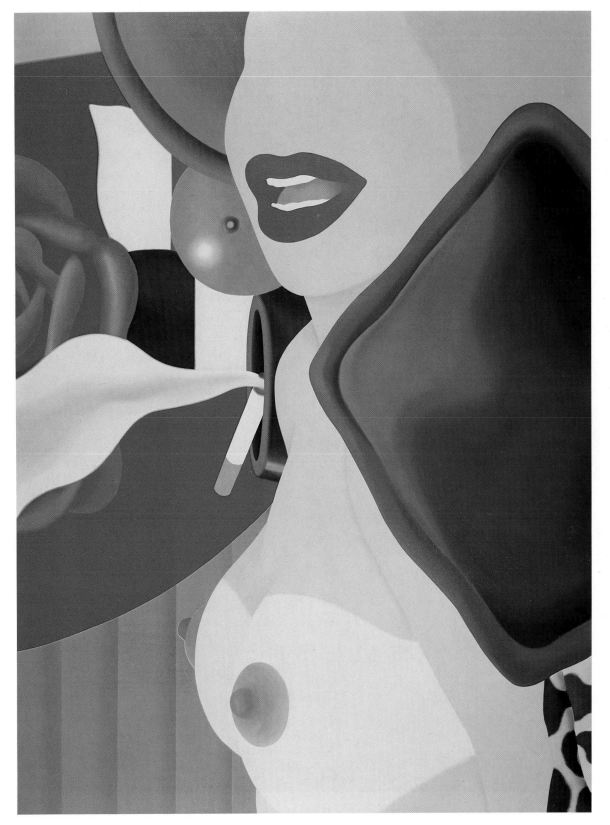

Colour Plate 13   Tom Wesselmann, *Great American Nude No. 99*, 1968, oil on canvas, 153 × 206 cm, Morton G. Neumann Family Collection, courtesy of Sidney Janis Gallery, New York.

Colour Plate 14   Giuseppe Arcimboldo, *Rudolf II as Vertumnus*, 1591, oil on canvas, 68 × 56 cm, Nationalmuseum, Stockholm, Baron von Essen Collection.

Colour Plate 15   John Constable, *The Leaping Horse*, full-scale sketch, 1824–25, 130 × 188 cm, Victoria and Albert Museum. *Photo*: J.C. Cooper Ltd.

Colour Plate 16   John Constable, *The Leaping Horse*, 1824–5, oil on canvas, 142 × 188 cm, Royal Academy, London.

Colour Plate 17   William Holman Hunt, *The Light of the World*, 1851–3 (retouched 1858), oil on canvas, 126 × 60 cm, Keble College, Oxford. *Photo*: By permission of the Warden and Fellows of Keble College, Oxford.

Colour Plate 18   William Holman Hunt, *The Awakening Conscience*, 1853–4, oil on canvas, 77 × 56 cm, Tate Gallery, London.

Colour Plate 19   Sir Charles Eastlake, *Christ Blessing Little Children*, 1839, oil on canvas, 79 × 103 cm, Manchester City Art Galleries.

Colour Plate 20   William Dyce, *Joash Shooting the Arrow of Deliverance*, 1844, oil on canvas, 78 × 110 cm, Hamburger Kunsthalle. *Photo*: Ralph Kleinhempel, Hamburg.

Colour Plate 21 John Everett Millais, *Christ in the Carpenter's Shop*, 1849–50, oil on canvas, 86 × 140 cm, Tate Gallery, London.

Colour Plate 23   Fra Angelico, *The Annunciation*, c. 1430–32, oil on panel with predella panels depicting scenes from the life of the Virgin, 192 × 192 cm, Museo del Prado, Madrid.

Colour Plate 22   Dante Gabriel Rossetti, *Ecce Ancilla Domini!*, 1849–50, oil on canvas, mounted on panel, 73 × 42 cm, Tate Gallery, London.

Colour Plate 24 Ford Madox Brown, *The Last of England*, 1852–3, oil on wood, 83 × 75 cm, Birmingham Museums and Art Gallery.

Colour Plate 25 William Holman Hunt, *Our English Coasts, 1852 (Strayed Sheep)*, 1852, oil on canvas, 43 × 58 cm, Tate Gallery, London.

Colour Plate 26   William Powell Frith, *Ramsgate Sands*, 1854, oil on canvas, 76 × 153 cm, Royal Collection. *Photo*: reproduced by gracious permission of Her Majesty the Queen.

Colour Plate 27   William Dyce, *Pegwell Bay : A Recollection of October 5th 1858*, 1860, oil on canvas, 64 × 89 cm, Tate Gallery, London.

Colour Plate 28   Operative Bricklayers' Society banner (Watford Branch), originally designed *c.*1865. *Photo*: National Museum of Labour History.

Colour Plate 29 Ford Madox Brown, *Work*, 1852–63, oil on canvas, 137 × 197 cm, Manchester City Art Galleries.

Colour Plate 30   Emily Mary Osborne, *Nameless and Friendless*, exh. 1857, oil on canvas, 88 × 103 cm, collection of Sir David Scott.

Colour Plate 31 Dante Gabriel Rossetti, *Found*, 1854–82, oil on canvas (unfinished), 90 × 77 cm, Delaware Art Museum, Samuel and Mary R. Bancroft Memorial Collection.

Centre

Right

Left

Colour Plate 32
Augustus Egg, *Past &
Present*, 1858, three
paintings, oil on
canvas, each
64 × 76 cm, Tate
Gallery, London.

Colour Plate 33   George Bernard O'Neill, *Public Opinion*, exh. 1863, oil on canvas, 93 × 62 cm, Leeds City Art Galleries. *Photo*: West Park Studios.

Colour Plate 34   Ford Madox Brown, *The Pretty Baa Lambs*, 1851, oil on panel, 61 × 76 cm, Birmingham Museums and Art Gallery.

Colour Plate 35   William Holman Hunt, *The Hireling Shepherd*, 1851–2, oil on canvas, 76 × 110 cm, Manchester City Art Galleries.

There is a willow grows aslant the
brook That shows his hoar leaves
in the glassy stream; There
with fantastic garlands
did she come. Of
crow-flowers,
nettles,
daisies,
and
long purples. There on the pendant
boughs her coronet weeds
Clambering to hang, an
envious sliver broke. When
down the weedy
trophies and herself
Fell in the
weeping
brook

Colour Plate 36 Arthur Hughes, *Ophelia*, 1852, oil on canvas, 69 × 124 cm, Manchester City Art Galleries.

Colour Plate 37 John Everett Millais, *Ophelia*, 1853, oil on canvas, 76 × 112 cm, Tate Gallery, London.

Colour Plate 38 John Everett Millais, *A Huguenot on St Bartholomew's Day*, 1851–2, oil on canvas, 93 × 62 cm, Makins Collection.

Colour Plate 39 Daniel Maclise, *Alfred the Great Disguised as a Minstrel in the Tent of Guthrum the Dane*, 1852, oil on canvas, 122 × 217 cm, Laing Gallery, Newcastle-upon-Tyne.

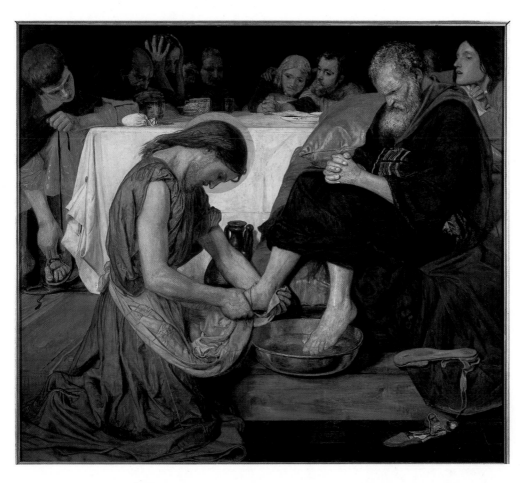

Colour Plate 40   Ford Madox Brown, *Jesus Washing Peter's Feet*, 1851–56, oil on canvas, 117 × 133 cm, Tate Gallery, London.

Colour Plate 41
Ford Madox Brown,
*Portrait of James
Leathart*, 1864, oil on
canvas, 33 × 28 cm,
Leathart family
collection.

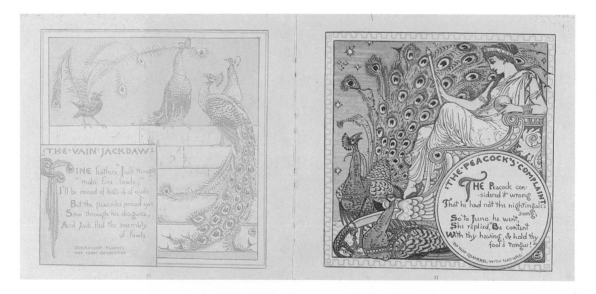

Colour Plate 42   Walter Crane, *The Vain Jackdaw and the Peacock's complaint*. Lithograph opening from *Baby's Own Aesop*, Frederick Warne and Co., 1887, 18 × 38 cm. *Photo*: courtesy of Colin Cunningham.

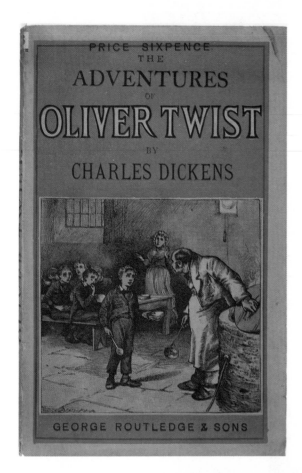

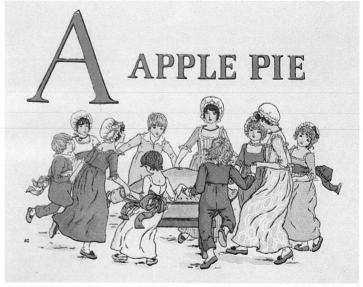

Colour Plate 43   Kate Greenaway, *A is for Apple Pie*, 1886, George Routledge, lithograph illustration. *Photo*: reproduced by permission of the London Borough of Camden, Local History Collection.

Colour Plate 44   Sir John Everett Millais (attrib.), cover illustration for *The Adventures of Oliver Twist* by Charles Dickens, 1890 edition, 22 × 14 cm, Routledge Railway Library. *Photo*: Cambridge University Library.

Colour Plate 45 Owen Jones, Chinese ornament, detail from painted porcelain. Lithograph from *The Grammar of Ornament*, Plate LXI, Day and Son, 1856.

Colour Plate 46   Amalgamated Society of Engineers Membership Certificate, 1851. *Photo*: courtesy of the Amalgamated Union of Engineering Workers.

Colour Plate 47   Amalgamated Society of Carpenters Membership Certificate, 1861. *Photo*: courtesy of National Museum of Labour History.

Colour Plate 48   Artist unknown, frontispiece for *In Darkest England & the Way Out* by William Booth, 1891.

Colour Plate 49   E.L. Blackburn, *Suburban and Rural Architecture*, 1869. Details for a pair of seven-roomed villas in the Italian style. *Photo*: by permission of the British Library Board.

Colour Plate 50   William Henry Hunt, *Primroses and Bird's Nest*, watercolour, 18 × 27 cm, Tate Gallery, London.

Colour Plate 51   Ford Madox Brown, *An English Afternoon, Hampstead : Scenery in 1853*, 1852–3, oil on canvas, 71 × 135 cm, Birmingham Museums and Art Gallery.

Colour Plate 52   James McNeill Whistler, *Nocturne in Blue and Silver–Chelsea* (also known as *Nocturne in Blue and Green*), 1871, oil on canvas, 50 × 59 cm, Tate Gallery, London.

Colour Plate 53   William Powell Frith, *The Railway Station*, 1862, oil on canvas, 115 × 253 cm, Royal Holloway College, University of London. *Photo*: Bridgeman Art Library.

Colour Plate 54   Frank Holl, *Newgate: Committed for Trial*, 1878, oil on canvas, 156 × 215 cm, Royal Holloway College, University of London. *Photo*: Bridgeman Art Gallery.

Colour Plate 55 Sir Luke Fildes, *Applicants for Admission to a Casual Labour Ward*, 1874, oil on canvas, 142 × 243 cm, Royal Holloway College, University of London. *Photo*: Bridgeman Art Gallery.

Colour Plate 57
James McNeill
Whistler, *Miss Cicely
Alexander : Harmony
in Grey and Green*,
1872–3, oil on canvas,
190 × 98 cm, Tate
Gallery, London.

Colour Plate 56
James McNeill
Whistler, *The White
Girl : Symphony in
White, No. 1*, 1862,
oil on canvas,
215 × 108 cm,
National Gallery of
Art, Washington,
Harris Whittemore
Collection.

Colour Plate 58   Sir Edward Burne-Jones, *King Cophetua and the Beggar Maid*, 1883–4, oil on canvas, 290 × 136 cm, Tate Gallery, London.

Colour Plate 60 James McNeill Whistler, *Nocturne in Black and Gold : the Falling Rocket*, 1875, oil on panel, 60 × 47 cm, Detroit Institute of Arts. Gift of Dexter M. Ferry Jr.

Colour Plate 59 James McNeill Whistler, *Nocturne in Blue and Gold : Old Battersea Bridge*, 1872–3, 67 × 50 cm, Tate Gallery, London.

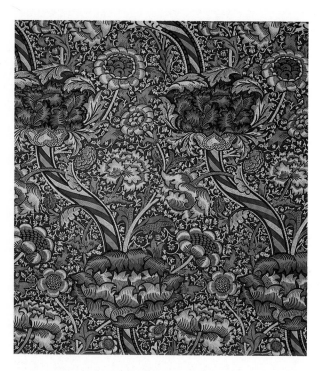

Colour Plate 61   William Morris, *Strawberry Thief*, 1883, printed fabric. *Photo*: by courtesy of the Trustees of the Victoria and Albert Museum.

Colour Plate 62   William Morris, *Wandle*, 1884, printed cotton. *Photo*: A.C. Cooper Ltd; by courtesy of the Victoria and Albert Museum.

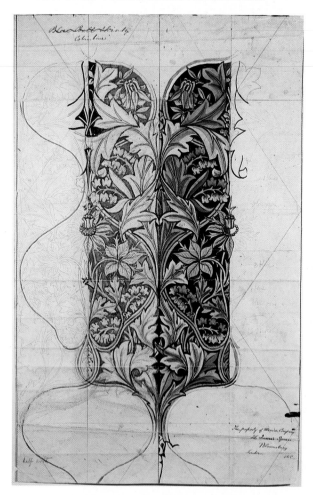

Colour Plate 63   William Morris, *Bluebell Chintz*, working drawing. *Photo*: A.C. Cooper Ltd; by courtesy of the Victoria and Albert Museum.

Colour Plate 64   William Morris, *Blackthorn wallpaper*, 1892. *Photo*: A.C. Cooper Ltd; by courtesy of the Victoria and Albert Museum.

Plate 1   Ritual mask from Elema
District, New Guinea, worn by
members of a secret society.
Reproduced by permission of the
Trustees of the British Museum.

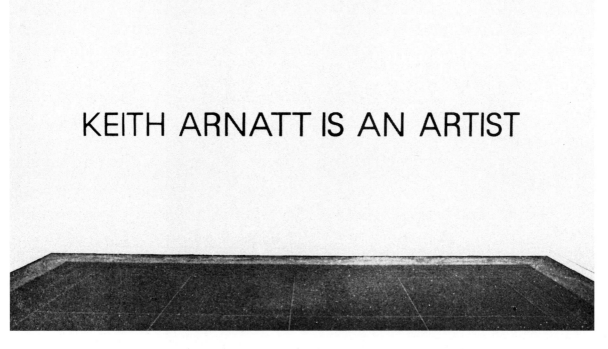

Plate 2   Keith Arnatt, *Keith Arnatt Is an Artist*, wall inscription, exhibited 1972 at the Tate Gallery,
London. *Photo*: Arts Council of Great Britain.

Plate 3   John Baldessari, . . . *No Ideas Have Entered This Work*, 1966–8, acrylic on canvas, 171 × 143 cm. *Photo*: By courtesy of the artist.

Plate 4   R. Mutt (Marcel Duchamp), *Fontaine (Fountain)*, 1917, industrially produced porcelain urinal. *Photo*: Philadelphia Museum of Art, Louise and Walter Arensberg Collection.

Plate 5

Plate 5 Artist unknown, jamb statues, Chartres Cathedral, west portals, *c.*1145–70, stone, over life size. *Photo*: James Austin.

Plate 6

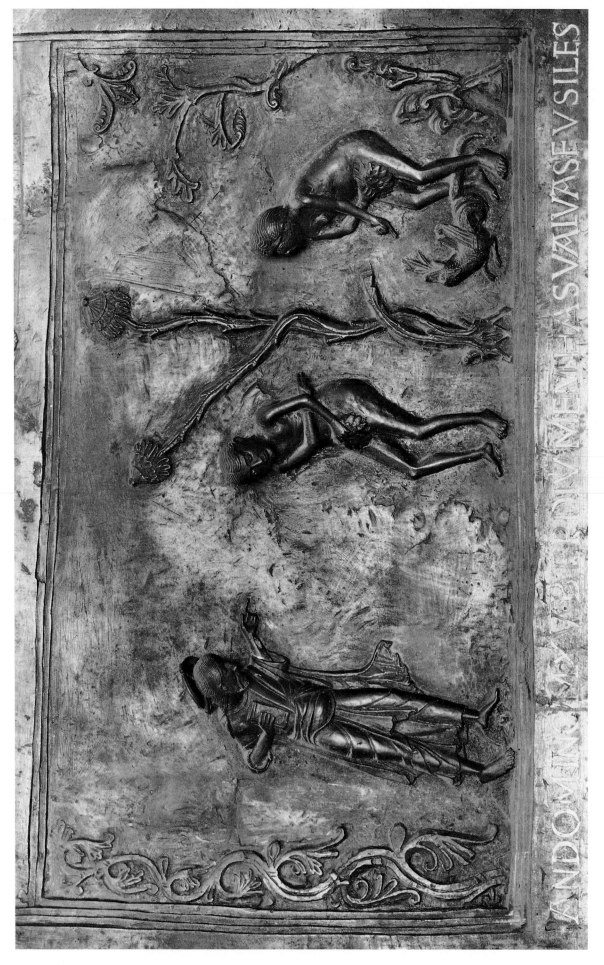

Plate 6 Artist unknown, *Adam and Eve Reproached by the Lord*, 1015, bronze, *c.*58 × 109 cm, detail of doors of Bishop Wernward, Hildesheim Cathedral, Germany. *Photo*: Bildarchiv, Foto Marburg.

Plate 7

Plate 7   Bonaventura Berlinghieri, *Saint Francis and Scenes from His Life*, 1235, tempera on panel, 160 × 123 cm, San Francesco, Pescia, Italy. *Photo*: Alinari, Florence.

Plate 8

Plate 8   Francesco Borromini, Sant'Ivo della Sapienza, Rome, 1642–50, view from courtyard. *Photo:* Alinari, Florence.

Plate 9

Plate 9   Étienne-Maurice Falconet, *Equestrian Monument to Peter the Great*, 1766–79, bronze and stone, over life size, Leningrad. *Photo*: Novosti Press Agency.

Plate 10

Plate 10   Christo Javacheff, *Wrapped Coast*, Little Bay, Australia, 1969, cloth over coastline, 1,000,000 sq. feet. *Photo*: Shunk-Kender, © Christo.

Plate 11

Plate 11 Claes Oldenburg, *Proposed Colossal Monument for Thames River: Thames 'Ball'*, 1967, crayon, ink and watercolour on postcard, 9 × 14 cm.
Photo: Carroll Janis Collection, New York.

Plate 12

Plate 12   Claes Oldenburg, *Proposed Colossal Monument for Park Avenue, New York : Good Humor Bar*,
1965, crayon and watercolour, 61 × 46 cm. *Photo*: Carroll Janis Collection, New York.

Plate 13

Plate 13 Claes Oldenburg, *Late Submission to the Chicago Tribune Architectural Competition of 1922: Clothespin*, 1967, crayon, pencil and watercolour on paper, 56 × 59 cm. *Photo*: Des Moines Center, gift of Gardner Cowles by exchange, and partial gift of Charles Cowles, 1972.

Plate 14

Plate 14   Donatello, *Pazzi Madonna*, ?*c.* 1420, marble, 75 × 70 cm, Staatliche Museen Preussischer Kulturbesitz, Berlin. *Photo*: Jörg P. Anders, Berlin.

Plate 15

Plate 15   Michelangelo, *Taddei Tondo*, *c.*1504, marble, diameter 117 cm, Royal Academy of Arts, London.

Plate 16

Plate 16 Michelangelo, *Last Judgement*, 1533–41, fresco, 210 × 140 cm, Sistine Chapel, Vatican. *Photo*: Alinari, Florence.

Plate 17

Plate 17 James Barry, *Grecian Harvest Home*, 1777–83, oil on canvas, 426 × 315 cm, Royal Society of Arts: copyright reserved. *Photo*: Paul Mellon Centre for Studies in British Art, London.

Plate 18

Plate 18   Nicolas Poussin, *Ordination*, 1647, oil on canvas, 118 × 177 cm, Duke of Sutherland Collection, on loan to the National Gallery of Scotland.

Plate 19

Plate 19 Hagesandros, Polydoros, and Athenodorus (three Rhodian sculptors), *The Death of the Priest Laocoön and his Sons*, *c*.42–21 BC, marble, height 244 cm, the Vatican Museum, Rome. *Photo*: Archivio Fotografico Monumenti Musei e Gallerie Pontificie, Vatican City, Rome.

Plate 20

Plate 20   Raphael, *Pope Julius II*, c.1512, oil on panel, 108 × 81 cm, National Gallery, London.

Plate 21

Plate 21 Thomas de Keyser, *Portrait of Constantijn Huygens and His Clerk*, 1627, oil on panel, 92 × 69 cm, National Gallery, London.

Plate 22

Plate 22   Sir Joshua
Reynolds, *Three Ladies
Adorning a Term of Hymen*,
1774, oil on canvas,
234 × 290 cm, Tate
Gallery, London.

Plate 23

Plate 23 Jan Molenaer,
The Dentist, 1630, oil on
canvas, 66 × 81 cm, Herzog
Anton Ulrich-Museum,
Brunswick. *Photo*: B.P.
Keiser.

Plate 24

Plate 24 Caravaggio, *The First Saint Matthew*, c.1598, oil on canvas, 223 × 183 cm, destroyed in WWII, formerly Kaiser Friedrich Museum, Berlin, No. 365. *Photo*: Bildarchiv, Foto Marburg.

Plate 25

Plate 25 Gustave Courbet, *The Stonebreakers*, 1849, oil on canvas, 165 × 238 cm, destroyed in WWII, formerly Gemäldegalerie, Dresden. *Photo:* Bildarchiv, Foto Marburg.

Plate 26 Artist unknown, *Bishop Odo Blessing the Food and Drink at the Feast of William the Conqueror*, scenes 43–44, Bayeux Tapestry, *c.*1073–83, wool embroidery on linen, 51 cm high, the whole tapestry 70 m long, Town Hall, Bayeux, France. *Photo*: Photographie Giraudon, Paris.

Plate 27

Plate 27   Harvey, '*It's the Way They Draw These Wretched Tables*', *The Bulletin*,
Sydney, Australia; reproduced as Fig. 7 in E. H. Gombrich (1982) *The Image and the
Eye*, Phaidon. *Photo*: By courtesy of the Australian Consolidated Press Ltd., Sydney.

Plate 28

Plate 28   Balthazar van der Ast, *Still-life with Shells*, before 1657, oil on panel, 30 × 47 cm, Museum Boymans-van Beuningen, Rotterdam.

Plate 29

Plate 29 Gustave Courbet, *Bouquet of Flowers*, 1855, oil on canvas, 84 × 109 cm, Kunstalle, Hamburg. *Photo*: Ralph Kleinhempel.

Plate 30

Plate 30 Floris van Dyck, *Breakfast Piece*, 1613, oil on panel, 50 × 77 cm, Franz Halsmuseum, Haarlem. *Photo*: Tom Haartsen.

Plate 31

Plate 31   Simon de Vliegher, *A Dutch Man-of-war and Various Vessels in a Breeze*, c.1642, oil on panel, 41 × 55 cm, National Gallery, London.

Plate 32

Plate 32 J.M.W. Turner, *The Egremont Sea Piece*, exhibited at the Royal Academy 1802, oil on canvas, 120 × 181 cm, Petworth House. *Photo*: The National Trust.

Plate 33

Plate 33   Gerrit Berckheyde, *View of the Grote Mart and Saint Bavo, Haarlem*, 1674, oil on canvas, 52 × 67 cm, National Gallery, London.

Plate 34

Plate 34   Hendrik Avercamp, *Winter Landscape*, before 1634, oil on panel, 78 × 132 cm, Rijksmuseum–Stichting, Amsterdam.

Plate 35

Plate 35   Evaristo Baschenis, *Still-life with Musical Instruments and a Statuette*, before 1677, oil on canvas, 87 × 155 cm, Accademia Carrara, Bergamo. *Photo*: Alinari, Florence.

Plate 36

Plate 36 William Powell Frith, *Derby Day*, 1856–8, oil on canvas, 102 × 224 cm, Tate Gallery, London.

Plate 37

Plate 37 John Ritchie, *Hampstead Heath*, 1859, oil on canvas, 83 × 135 cm, private collection.

Plate 38

Plate 38   Henry Alexander Bowler, *The Doubt: 'Can These Dry Bones Live?'*, exhibited 1855, oil on canvas, 60 × 50 cm, Tate Gallery, London.

Plate 39   Raphael, *Charge to Saint Peter*, *c*.1515, tempera and charcoal on paper, 345 × 535 cm, Victoria and Albert Museum, London, Crown Copyright.

Plate 40   William Holman Hunt, *The Finding of the Saviour in the Temple*, 1854–5 and 1856–60, oil on canvas, 46 × 70 cm, Birmingham Museum and Art Gallery.

Plate 42   William Holman Hunt, *The Shadow of Death*, 1870–3, retouched 1886, tempera and oil on canvas, 214 × 168 cm, City of Manchester Art Galleries.

Plate 41   Dante Gabriel Rossetti, study of Virgin in *Ecce Ancilla Domini!*, *c*.1849, drawing, 18 × 13 cm, Tate Gallery, London.

Plate 43

Plate 43   Dante Gabriel Rossetti, *The Seed of David*, 1854–64, oil on canvas, triptych, central panel
225 × 150 cm, side panels 183 × 61 cm, Llandaff Cathedral, Cardiff. *Photo*: James Marks, Woodmansterne Ltd.

Plate 44

Plate 44   William Dyce, *The Holy Trinity and Saints*, study for the fresco in All Saints Church, Margaret Street, London, *c.*1849, oil on canvas, 87 × 39 cm, Victoria and Albert Museum, London, Crown Copyright.

Plate 45   William Dyce, *Pegwell Bay*, 1857, watercolour sketch, 25 × 35 cm, private collection.
Photo: Studio Morgan.

Plate 46   William Dyce, *Man of Sorrows*, 1860, oil on canvas, 35 × 48 cm, National Gallery of Scotland, Edinburgh.

Plate 47

Plate 47 Gustave Doré, *Lambeth Gasworks*, wood engraving from William Blanchard Jerrold, *London : a Pilgrimage*, Grant and Co., 1872. *Photo*: From 1970 reprint of the 1872 edition, published by Dover Publications Inc., New York, opposite page 40.

Plate 48

Plate 48   Hubert von Herkomer, *On Strike*, 1891, oil on canvas, 228 × 126 cm, Royal Academy of Arts, London.

Plate 49   Gustave Doré, *Mixing the Malt*, wood engraving from William Blanchard Jerrold, *London : a Pilgrimage*, Grant and Co., 1872. *Photo*: From 1970 reprint of the 1872 edition, published by Dover Publications Inc., New York, page 130.

Plate 50   Ford Madox Brown, sketch for *Work*, ?1852 or 1864, watercolour and pencil, 20 × 28 cm, based on the now lost original pen and ink sketch, 1852, City of Manchester Art Galleries.

Plate 51

Plate 51   Daniel Maclise, *Peter the Great at Deptford Dockyard*, 1857, oil on canvas, 150 × 225 cm, Royal Holloway College, University of London.

Plate 52   Elizabeth Thompson (Lady Butler), *Calling the Roll after an Engagement, Crimea (The Roll Call)*, 1879, oil on canvas, 90 × 180 cm, Her Majesty the Queen's Collection.

Plate 53   May Morris, 'Honeysuckle' wallpaper, 1883, Victoria and Albert Museum, London. *Photo*: A.C. Cooper Ltd.

Plate 54

Plate 54　Elizabeth Siddal, *Lady Clare*, ?1854–7, watercolour, 34 × 25 cm, private collection.

Plate 56 Daniel Gabriel Rossetti, *The Girlhood of Mary Virgin*, 1848–9, oil on canvas, 83 × 65 cm, Tate Gallery, London.

Plate 55 George Elgar Hicks, *Woman's Mission : Companion of Manhood*, 1863, oil on canvas, 76 × 64 cm, Tate Gallery, London.

Plate 57   Richard Redgrave, *The Outcast*, 1851, oil on canvas, 79 × 104 cm, Royal Academy of Arts, London.

Plate 58   William Hogarth, *Before*, 1736, engraving, 37 × 30 cm. *Photo*: Reproduced by permission of the Trustees of the British Museum.

Plate 59   William Hogarth, *After*, 1736, engraving, 37 × 30 cm. *Photo*: Reproduced by permission of the Trustees of the British Museum.

Plate 60

Plate 60   William Holman Hunt, *The Children's Holiday (Portrait of Mrs Thomas Fairbairn and her Children)*, 1864–5, oil on canvas, 214 × 147 cm, Torbay Borough Council, Torre Abbey Collection, Torquay.

Plate 61

Plate 61 William Holman Hunt, *Christ and the Two Marys (The Risen Christ with the Two Marys in the Garden of Joseph of Aramathea)*, 1847, oil on canvas, 118 × 94 cm, Art Gallery of South Australia, Adelaide, D'Auvergne Boxall bequest fund, 1964.

Plate 62

Plate 62 Richard Redgrave, *The Seamstress*, 1846, oil on canvas, 63 × 75 cm, The Forbes Magazine Collection, New York. *Photo*: Otto E. Nelson.

Plate 64   George Morland, *The Fair Penitent*, 1789, engraved by John Raphael Smith. *Photo*: Reproduced by permission of the Trustees of the British Museum.

Plate 63   John Everett Millais, *Virtue and Vice*, 1853, pen and sepia ink, 13 × 18 cm, private collection.

Plate 65

Plate 65 Sir Charles Eastlake, *Christ Lamenting over Jerusalem*, 1841, oil on canvas, 98 × 148 cm, Glasgow Art Gallery and Museum

Plate 67 Thomas P. Hall, *One Touch of Nature Makes the Whole World Kin*, 1867, oil on canvas, 64 × 76 cm. *Photo*: from Wood, C. (1976) *Victorian Panorama : Paintings of Victorian Life*, Faber and Faber, p. 203; reproduced by kind permission of the author.

Plate 66 George Bernard O'Neill, *Gran's Treasures*, c.1866, oil on canvas, 35 × 28 cm, Guildhall Art Library, City of London. *Photo*: Godfrey New Photographics Ltd.

Plate 68 John Everett Millais, *Portrait of Mrs Coventry Patmore*, exhibited 1852, oil on wood, 19 × 20 cm, Cambridge, Fitzwilliam Museum.

Plate 69 Robert Brathwaite Martineau, *Kit's First Writing Lesson*, exhibited 1852, oil on canvas, 51 × 69 cm, Tate Gallery, London.

Plate 70

Plate 70   Daniel Maclise, *The Death of Nelson*, 1858–66, waterglass painting, 363 × 1410 cm, Royal Gallery, House of Lords, London. *Photo*: PSA Photographic Library.

Plate 71   Charles Allston Collins, *May in the Regent's Park*, 1851, oil on panel, 44 × 68 cm, Tate Gallery, London.

Plate 72   George E. Hicks, *Dividend Day at the Bank of England*, 1859, oil on canvas, 90 × 135 cm. Reproduced by permission of the Governor and Company of the Bank of England.

Plate 73

Plate 73   William Holman Hunt, *A Converted British Family Sheltering a Priest from the Persecution of the Druids*, 1850, oil on canvas, 119 × 131 cm, Ashmolean Museum, Oxford.

Plate 74

Plate 74   Ford Madox Brown, *Geoffrey Chaucer Reading the 'Legend of Custance' to Edward III and His Court, at the Palace of Sheen, on the Anniversary of the Black Prince's Forty-fifth Birthday*, 1845–51, oil on canvas, 372 × 296 cm, Art Gallery of New South Wales, Sydney, Australia.

Plate 75

Plate 75   After William Holman Hunt, *The Light of the World* (1851–3) (see Colour plate 17), engraving by W.H. Simmons, published by E. Gambart and Co. 1860, 79 × 31 cm. Reproduced by permission of the Trustees of the British Museum, London.

Plate 76   After Sir Edwin Landseer, *The Monarch of the Glen* (1851), engraving by
Thomas Landseer, published by Henry Graves and Co. 1852, 60 × 59 cm. Reproduced
by permission of the Trustees of the British Museum.

Plate 77   Detail of Plate 76.

Plate 78   After Daniel Maclise,
The Death of Nelson (1874) (see
Plate 70), engraving published by
the Art Union of London, 1876,
45 × 123 cm, detail. Reproduced
by permission of the Trustees of
the British Museum.

Plate 79   Detail of Plate 80.

Plate 80

Plate 80   After Myles Birket Foster, *The Old Chair-mender*, wood engraving by the Dalziel brothers from *Pictures of the English Landscape*, Routledge, Warne and Routledge, 1863, 18 × 14 cm. *Photo*: Mary Evans Picture Library.

Plate 81   S. Luke Fildes, *Houseless and Hungry*, wood engraving, 20 × 30 cm, from the *Graphic*, 1869.
Photo: Reproduced by permission of the British Library Board.

Plate 82   Detail of Plate 81.

Plate 83   After John Everett
Millais, *Ophelia* (1853) (see
Colour plate 37), mezzo-tint with
engraving, published by Henry
Graves and Co. 1866, 51 × 85 cm,
detail. Reproduced by permission
of the Trustees of the British
Museum.

Plate 84   Detail of Plate 86.

Plate 85

Plate 85   William Morris and Sir Edward Coley Burne-Jones, a page from *The Works of Geoffrey Chaucer Now Newly Printed . . .* , wood engraving with letterpress, Kelmscott Press, 1896, 40 × 28 cm. *Photo*: Reproduced by permission of the British Library Board.

Plate 86　After William Powell Frith, *The Railway Station* (1862) (see Colour plate 53), engraving by Francis Holl, published by Henry Graves 1866, 50 × 110 cm. Reproduced by permission of the Trustees of the British Museum.

Plate 87　After William Holman Hunt, *The Finding of the Saviour in the Temple* (1854–5 and 1856–60) (see Plate 40), engraving by A.T.M. Blanchard, published by E. Gambart and Co. 1867, 39 × 64 cm. Reproduced by permission of the Trustees of the British Museum.

Plate 88   After Thomas Faed, *The Last of the Clan* (1865), engraving by W.H. Simmons, published by Henry Graves 1868, 62 × 79 cm. Reproduced by permission of the Trustees of the British Museum.

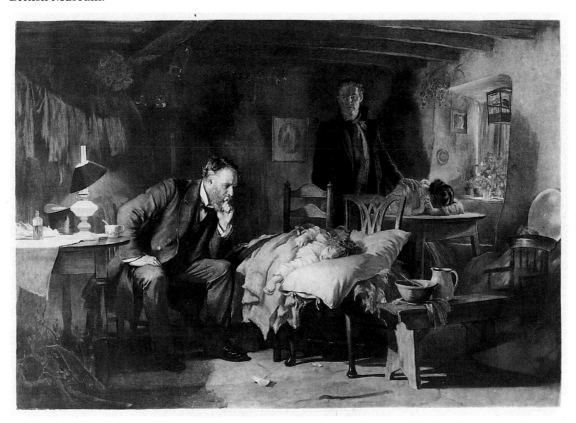

Plate 89   After S. Luke Fildes, *The Doctor* (exhibited at the RA 1891), engraving published by Agnews 1893, 59 × 88 cm, Victoria and Albert Museum, London.

Plate 90 After William Powell Frith, *Derby Day* (1856–8) (see Plate 36), engraving published by E. Gambart 1858, 50 × 111 cm, detail, British Museum, London.

Plate 91 After John Everett Millais, *Bubbles* (1886), engraving first reproduced by the *Illustrated London News*, then sold to Messrs. Pears. *Photo*: Mansell Collection, London.

Plate 92 S. Luke Fildes, '*Under the Trees*', wood engraving, from Charles Dickens, *The Mystery of Edwin Drood, a Novel*, Chapman and Hall, 1870.

Plate 94 John Everett Millais, 'Mrs Gresham and Miss Dunstable', wood engraving, from Anthony Trollope, *Framley Parsonage*, 1862. *Photo*: Reproduced by permission of the British Library Board.

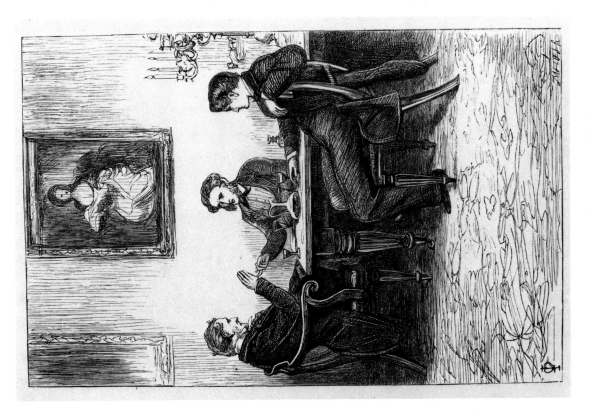

Plate 93 John Everett Millais, 'Over their Wine', wood engraving from Anthony Trollope, *Orley Farm*, 1862. *Photo*: Reproduced by permission of the British Library Board.

Plate 95

Plate 95   Gustave Doré, title-page from William Blanchard Jerrold, *London: a Pilgrimage*, Grant and Co.,
1872, wood engraving, 31 × 23 cm. *Photo*: Reproduced by permission of the British Library Board.

Plate 96   Gustave Doré, '*Under the Arches*', wood engraving from William Blanchard Jerrold, *London : a Pilgrimage*, Grant and Co., 1872, 11 × 16 cm. *Photo*: From 1970 reprint of the 1872 edition, published by Dover Publications Inc., New York.

Plate 97   Gustave Doré, '*Seven Days, Seven Nights . . .*', from Samuel Taylor Coleridge, *The Rime of the Ancient Mariner*, 1875, detail. *Photo*: From 1979 edition, Arno Press/ Mayflower Books, New York.

Plate 98

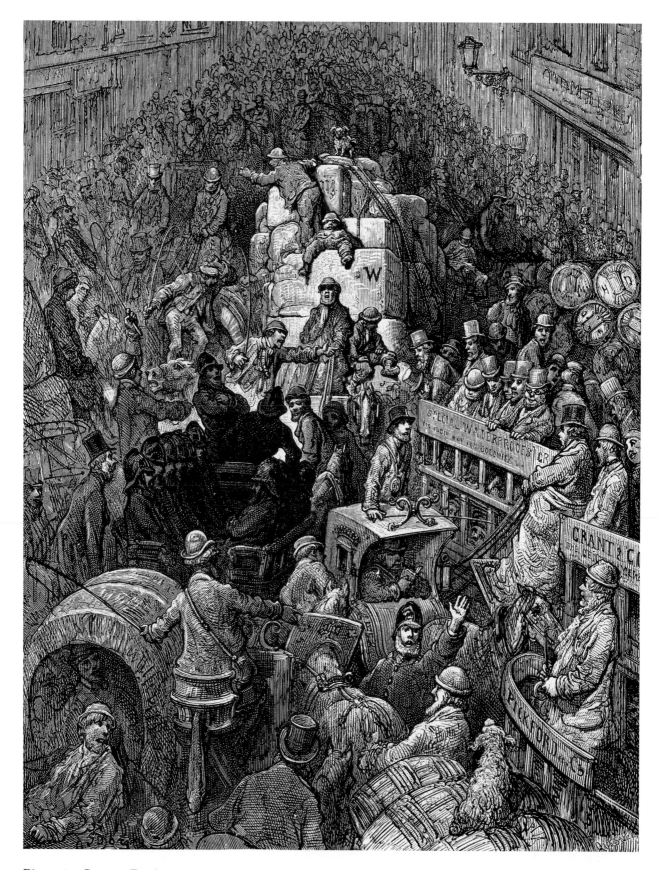

Plate 98   Gustave Doré, '*A City Thoroughfare*', wood engraving from William Blanchard Jerrold, *London : A Pilgrimage*, Grant and Co., 1872, 31 × 23 cm. *Photo*: From 1970 reprint of the 1872 edition, published by Dover Publications Inc., New York.

Plate 99

Plate 99 John Everett Millais, *Cherry Ripe*, coloured lithograph, 67 × 45 cm, from the *Graphic*, Christmas issue, 1880. *Photo*: By courtesy of the Syndics of the Cambridge University Library.

Plate 100

Plate 100   Certificate of the United Society of Boiler Makers and Iron and Steel Ship Builders, 1929.
Photo: National Museum of Labour History.

Plate 101

Plate 101 Certificate of the United Operative Plumbers' Association, ?1861. *Photo*: National Museum of Labour History.

Plate 102

Plate 102   Certificate of the Operative Bricklayers' Society, 1895. *Photo*: National Museum of Labour History.

Plate 103

Plate 103   Drawing in commemoration of the Great Strike, September 1889. *Photo*: National Museum of Labour History.

Plate 104

Plate 104   Walter Crane, *The Triumph of Labour*, engraving commemorating Labour Day, 1891. *Photo*: Museum of Labour History.

Plate 105 Myles Birkett Foster, *The Milkmaid*, 1860, oil on canvas, 29 × 44 cm, Victoria and Albert Museum, London.

Plate 106 Henry Wallis, *The Stonebreaker*, 1857, oil on canvas, 61 × 79 cm, Birmingham Museums and Art Gallery.

Plate 107

Plate 107 Hubert von Herkomer, *Hard Times*, 1885, oil on canvas, 85 × 111 cm, City of Manchester Art Galleries.

Plate 108   James Abbott McNeill Whistler, *Wapping on Thames*, 1861, oil on canvas, 70 × 100 cm, John Hay Whitney Collection, National Gallery of Art, Washington DC.

Plate 109   James Abbott McNeill Whistler, *Harmony in Blue and Gold : The Peacock Room*, 1876–7 (with *La Princesse du pays de la porcelaine* above fireplace), oil colour and gold on leather and wood, room dimensions 4.2 × 10 × 6 m. (Courtesy of the Freer Gallery of Art, Smithsonian Institution, Washington DC).

Plate 110

Plate 110   Gustave Doré, *Refuge – Applying for Admittance in London*, wood engraving from William Blanchard Jerrold, *London: a Pilgrimage*, Grant and Co., 1872. *Photo*: From 1970 reprint of the 1872 edition, published by Dover Publications Inc., New York.

Plate 111   Kelmscott Manor, the panelled room, with some of Morris's furniture. *Photo*: BBC Hulton Picture Library.

Plate 112   A typical Victorian drawing room, *c*.1867. *Photo*: BBC Hulton Picture Library.

Plate 113   Philip Webb, The Red House, Bexley Heath, built for William Morris, 1859. *Photo*: National Monuments Record.

Plate 114   The Red House, Bexley Heath, entrance hall. *Photo*: Country Life; reproduced by kind permission of Mr and Mrs Hollamby.

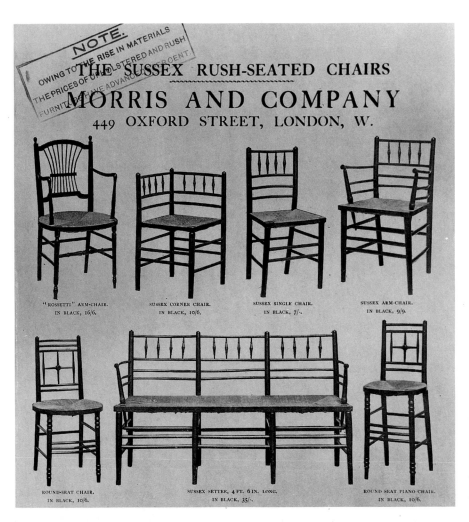

Plate 115 Morris and Co., page from company's catalogue showing the Sussex rush seated chairs. *Photo*: The William Morris Gallery, Walthamstow, London.

Plate 116 Kelmscott Press colophon, woodcut, designed by William Morris. *Photo*: The William Morris Gallery, Walthamstow, London.

Plate 117

Plate 117 William Morris's four-poster bed, with valance and curtains embroidered by May Morris and bedcover embroidered by Jane Morris; Morris wallpaper in background. *Photo*: A.F. Kersting.

Plate 118

Plate 118 Wightwick Manor, Staffordshire (West Midlands since 1974), the Great Parlour, built 1887–93, decorated and furnished by Morris and Co.
Photo: Country Life.

Plate 119

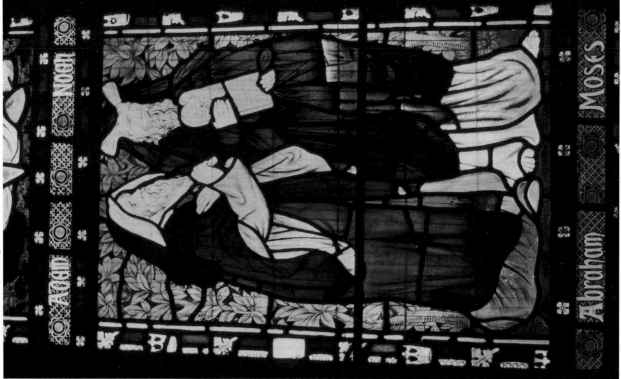

Plate 119   William
Morris, east window, All
Saints Church, Middleton
Cheney, details. *Photo*:
Charles Sewter, by
courtesy of the Whitworth
Art Gallery.